Festival Foods

Jenny Vaughan and
Penny Beauchamp

Heinemann Library
Chicago, Illinois

© 2004 Heinemann Library
a division of Reed Elsevier Inc.
Chicago, Illinois

Customer Service 888-454-2279

Visit our website at
www.heinemannlibrary.com

Produced for Heinemann Library by
Discovery Books Ltd.
Designed by Jo Hinton-Malivoire
and Rob Norridge
Illustrations by Nicholas Beresford-Davies
Picture Research by Laura Durman
Originated by Dot Gradations Ltd.
Printed in China by WKT Company Limited

08 07 06 05 04
10 9 8 7 6 5 4 3 2 1

Library of Congress Cataloging-in-Publication Data
Vaughan, Jenny.
   Festival foods / Jenny Vaughan and Penny
Beauchamp.
       p. cm. -- (World of recipes)
Summary: Presents recipes for foods
associated with various festivals and holidays
around the world.
   ISBN 1-4034-4699-7 (hardcover)
 1. Holiday cookery--Juvenile literature. 2.
Cookery, International--Juvenile literature. 3.
Fasts and feasts--Juvenile literature. [1.
Holiday cookery. 2. Cookery, International.]
I. Beauchamp, Penny. II. Title. TX739.V38
2004
   745.594'16--dc22
                              2003018010

Acknowledgments
The author and publishers are grateful to
the following for permission to reproduce
copyright material: p. 5 Patrick Ward/Corbis;
p. 28, 29 Steve Lee; all other photographs by
Terry Benson.

Cover photographs reproduced with
permission of Terry Benson.

Every effort has been made to contact
copyright holders of any material reproduced
in this book. Any omissions will be rectified
in subsequent printings if notice is given to
the publisher.

Contents

Key

* easy

** medium

*** difficult

Some words are shown in bold, **like this.** You can find out what they mean by looking in the glossary.

F stival Recip s

What is a festival?

A festival is a time when people celebrate an important event. Whole families or groups of friends often eat together as part of the celebration. The food they eat is something special, and usually there is plenty of it.

Many of the foods eaten at festivals are made using traditional recipes. The recipes in this book are from the countries shown in yellow on the map above.

Festivals around the world

There are many different festivals celebrated all over the world. Some of the best-known festivals are linked to religions, such as Christmas and Easter for Christians.

Other festivals celebrate special days, such as the New Year—but the New Year may not always begin on

4

January 1. For example, the Chinese New Year falls in early spring, while in the Hindu religion, the New Year falls in October or November. It is celebrated at the festival of *Divali* (see page 42). The Jewish New Year, *Rosh Hashanah*, also falls at around this time of the year.

Some festivals are unique to only one town or village. Other festivals, though, vary in the way they are celebrated in many different places at the same time. Family occasions, such as weddings or birthdays, are also a kind of festival. There are thousands of festivals all over the world, with an enormous variety of foods that are prepared especially for these occasions.

Fasts

A fast is the opposite of a festival. It is a more solemn time when people give up certain foods, or even all food, depending on their religion or custom. During Lent, many

Women carry offerings of food during a festival in Bali, Indonesia.

Christians do not eat meat or rich foods until Easter. Muslims keep to a fast that lasts throughout Ramadan, the ninth month of the Islamic year. During this time, Muslims may not eat or drink between sunrise and sunset. Ramadan ends with a festival called *Eid-ul-Fitr* during which special foods are eaten. Many fasting periods either begin or end with a special meal.

Ingredients

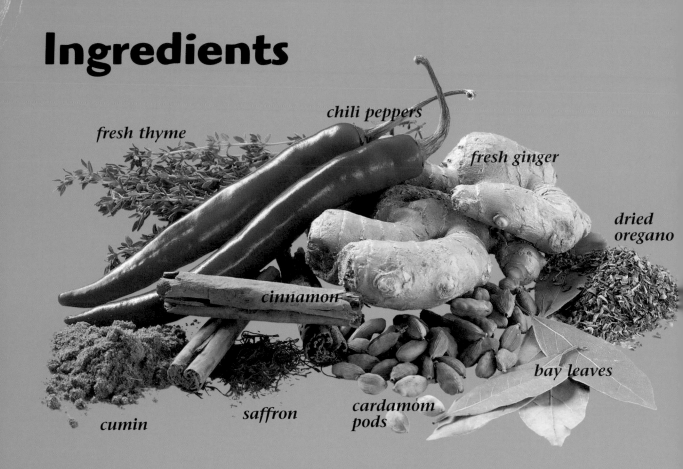

fresh thyme

chili peppers

fresh ginger

dried oregano

cinnamon

bay leaves

cumin

saffron

cardamom pods

Special foods

Festivals are special times, and the food that goes with them is special, too. Festival recipes often include foods that at one time were too expensive for people to eat very often.

Spices

Spices used to be expensive because in many parts of the world they had to be transported hundreds of miles across the sea. Spices were only used to give food a unique taste on important occasion, such as during a festival. Some spices, such as cumin or cardamom, are sold as seeds or pods. They can also be ground up to make a powder. Cinnamon is sold in sticks made from the bark of a tree. Most spices have a strong flavor, so you do not need to use very much of them.

Saffron

One of the most expensive spices is saffron. It is made from the orange-colored **stigmas** inside a special kind of crocus flower. Luckily, you usually only need to use a small amount of this spice. If you cannot get saffron, use a drop or two of yellow food coloring instead. This will not flavor the food, but it will give you the right yellow color.

Ginger

Ginger is a spicy root that can be used in both sweet and savory dishes. Some of the recipes in this book use fresh ginger. This is a root that must be **peeled** and either finely **chopped** or **grated** before it is used. Other recipes require ginger that has been dried and ground into a powder.

Chili peppers

A dish that contains chili peppers will always taste spicy. Chili peppers come in a variety of colors and sizes. Some are extremely spicy while others have a much milder flavor. Always be very careful when you are handling chili peppers. Never rub your eyes or nose, as the chili oil left on your fingers will make your skin sting.

Herbs

Herbs are used to add a flavor to food. Thyme is a Mediterranean herb that thrives in hot, dry conditions. Like most other herbs, it can be used either fresh or dried. When herbs are dried, it often makes their flavor stronger. Dried oregano is frequently **sprinkled** over pizzas. Bay leaves tend to be used to flavor soups and stews. In the past, people would only have used the herbs that they could pick near their homes, but today we can buy fresh or dried herbs from all over the world.

Before You Start

Kitchen rules

There are a few basic rules you should always follow when you are cooking.

- Ask an adult if you can use the kitchen.
- Some cooking processes, especially **frying**, and those using **boiling** water or syrup, can be dangerous. When you see this sign, always ask an adult for help.
- Wipe down any work surfaces before you start cooking and then wash your hands.
- Wear an apron to protect your clothes, and tie back long hair.
- Be very careful when using sharp knives.
- Never leave pan handles sticking out over the stove or countertop because you might bump into them and knock the pan over.
- Always wear oven mitts to lift things in and out of the oven.
- Wash fruit and vegetables before you use them.

How long will it take?

Some of the recipes in this book are quick and easy to make, while others are more difficult and may take longer. The stripe across the top of the right-hand page of each recipe tells you how long it will take to prepare each dish. It also shows you how difficult the dish is to make. Every recipe is marked as being
* (easy), ** (medium), or *** (difficult).

Quantities and measurements

You can see how many people each recipe will serve by looking at the stripe across the top of the right-hand page. You can multiply the quantities if you are cooking for more people, or divide them if you want to make less food.

Ingredients in recipes can be measured in different ways. Metric measurements use grams, liters, and milliliters. Imperial measurements use cups and ounces. This book lists both metric and imperial measurements.

In the recipes, you will see the following abbreviations:

tbsp = tablespoon   oz = ounce   in. = inch
tsp = teaspoon   lb = pound   ml = milliliter
cm = centimeter   g = gram

Utensils

To cook the following recipes, you will need these utensils (as well as essentials, such as spoons, plates, and bowls):

- aluminum foil
- baking tray
- **baking parchment**
- cake rack
- **chopping** board
- **colander**
- double boiler
- food processor or blender
- frying pan (with a lid)
- grater
- measuring cup
- omelette pan (nonstick)
- **ovenproof** dish about 6- x 9-in. (16- x 23-cm)
- square and round 8-in (20-cm) nonstick pie and cake pans
- pastry brush
- rolling pin and a pastry board
- 2-quart saucepan
- **slotted spoon**
- smaller nonstick saucepans
- **sieve**
- sharp knife
- **spatula**
- **whisk**

 Always be very careful when using kitchen knives.

Savory Dumplings (China)

Dumplings are often served during the festivities that mark the Chinese New Year. A festival is a time to celebrate, so food is prepared in advance to be eaten later.

What you need

1 green onion
Fresh ginger root,
    about ¼-in. (1-cm) long
1½ cups (300g) *pak choi*,
    or Chinese leaves
½ lb (250g) minced pork
1 tbsp soy sauce
1⅔ cups (175g) flour
Water

What you do

1 Wash the onion, cut off the root, and **chop** finely.

(!) **2** **Peel** and chop the ginger root very finely.

3 Chop the *pak choi* or Chinese leaves very finely.

(!) **4** Bring a pan of water to a **boil**. Add the *pak choi* and boil for 3 minutes. **Drain** the leaves through a **sieve**, **rinse** them under cold running water, and spread them out on paper towels.

5 Using your clean hands, thoroughly mix the **minced** pork, green onion, *pak choi*, ginger, and **soy sauce** together. Wash your hands.

6 Put the flour in the bowl and make a **well** in the middle. Gradually add ½ cup (115ml) water, stirring all the time with a fork to make a sticky **dough**.

7 **Knead** the dough on a floured board for 5–10 minutes, until it is smooth and stretchy. Roll it into a sausage shape with your hands.

8 Cut the dough into 16 equal pieces and roll out each one to make a thin circle. Place a teaspoonful of filling on each circle.

9 Fold each circle in half, pressing the sides firmly together. Use a fork to seal the edges.

⚠ 10 Bring a large pan of water to a boil. Drop 2 or 3 dumplings into it and cook them for 20 minutes. Take them out with a **slotted spoon.**

11 Cook the rest of the dumplings in batches of 2 or 3 at a time. (If you put too many in the pan, they will stick together.) Serve with soy sauce.

11

Pescado en Escabeche (Puerto Rico)

Puerto Rico is an island in the Caribbean Sea that lies between the continents of North and South America. This recipe is made during the week before Easter.

What you need

1 lb (400g) cod, haddock, or hake, with bones removed
¼ cup (30g) flour
¼ tsp paprika
¼ cup (60ml) olive oil
¼ of a mild onion
A small garlic clove
6 peppercorns
1 large bay leaf
Salt and pepper
2 tbsp (30ml) white wine vinegar

What you do

1 Cut the fish into 4 equal pieces, each about the size of a deck of cards.

2 Place the fish pieces on a plate and **sift** the flour onto them. Make sure they are well-covered with flour.

3 **Sprinkle** the fish with paprika.

4 Heat 2 tbsp of olive oil in a frying pan. **Fry** one piece of fish for 4 minutes on each side. Do not cook the fish too long, or it will start to fall apart when you lift it from the pan. Use a **spatula** to remove the fish from the pan.

5 Allow the fish to dry on paper towels. Repeat with the other three pieces of fish.

6 **Slice** the onion and garlic into thin strips.

7 Put the fish pieces in the bottom of a shallow pan that measures about 6- x 9-in. (16- x 23-cm). Sprinkle the onion, garlic, and peppercorns on top. Tear each bay leaf into 2 or 3 pieces and place between the fish pieces.

8 Sprinkle salt and pepper over the fish and vegetables.

9 **Whisk** the remaining oil with the vinegar and pour it over the fish. Cover the dish and keep it in the refrigerator until you are ready to serve it. **Baste** the fish occasionally with the oil and vinegar. Before serving, remove the bay leaves.

13

Ramadan Soup (Morocco)

This dish, called *harira* in Morocco, is a cross between a soup and a stew. It is made during Ramadan, a fast that lasts for the entire ninth month of the Muslim year. Muslims do not eat or drink between sunrise and sunset during Ramadan, and *harira* makes a filling meal that is especially welcome after a day of fasting.

What you need

½ lb (200g) lean lamb
1 onion
½ cup (115g) canned chickpeas, **drained**
2 tbsp olive oil
14 oz (400g) canned, chopped tomatoes, including the juice
½ cup (115g) dried red lentils
¼ cup (60g) long grain rice
1 tbsp tomato **purée**
¼ of a red pepper, chopped
Juice from 1 lemon
1 tbsp chopped fresh coriander
4 cups (1 liter) water

What you do

1 **Chop** the lamb into pieces of ½ x ½ in. (2 x 2 cm).

2 **Peel** and **slice** the onion.

3 **Rinse** and drain the chickpeas.

(!) 4 Heat the oil in a large pan. **Fry** the lamb for about 5 minutes, until it is lightly browned on all sides.

5 Add the onion and cook slowly. When it is soft, add all the other ingredients except the coriander.

6 Add 4 cups (1 liter) of water and bring the soup to a **boil. Simmer** for about 30 minutes, until the rice and lentils are **tender.**

7 Add the coriander and simmer for another 5 minutes. Serve hot.

N w Y ar Om l tt (Iran)

This omelette recipe is from ancient Persia, the country that is now called Iran. It is made for a New Year festival that dates back more than 1,000 years. Persian omelettes are unusual because they are frequently **baked** in the oven instead of being **fried** in a pan.

What you need

2 green onions
1 leek
¼ cup (40g) fresh spinach leaves
1 **sprig** parsley
1 tbsp fresh oregano and fresh thyme, mixed
6 large eggs
Salt and black pepper
2 tbsp (25g) butter

What you do

1 **Preheat** the oven to 325°F (170°C).

2 Wash the vegetables and dry them on paper towels.

3 Remove any damaged outer leaves from the green onions and the leek. Cut off the roots and green shoots.

4 **Chop** the green onions, leek, spinach, and herbs very finely.

5 **Beat** the eggs in a large bowl.

6 Mix the vegetables into the eggs. **Season** with salt and pepper.

7 **Grease** an **ovenproof** dish with butter. The exact size of the dish is not important, but it should be about 8 in. (20 cm) across. A round, nonstick cake pan is ideal.

8 Pour the egg mixture into the dish and cover it with aluminum foil.

(!) 9 Bake for 30 minutes, and then remove the foil. Cook for another 10 minutes, until the egg has set and the mixture is brown on top.

Fanesca (Ecuador)

This soup is eaten during Lent in the South American country of Ecuador, where many people are Roman Catholics. Many Catholics do not eat meat during Lent, and so this fish recipe is popular. Dried salt cod, called *bacalao*, is traditionally used in this dish. It can be difficult to find. Fresh cod or haddock can be used for this recipe instead.

What you need

1 onion
1 garlic clove
2 tbsp (25g) butter
1½ tsp dried oregano
1½ tsp ground cumin
Salt and freshly ground
   black pepper
½ cup (100g) long grain
   rice
1 cup (250g) mix of
   frozen broad beans,
   corn, pinto beans,
   and peas
2¼ cups (500ml)
   vegetable stock
2 level tbsp cornstarch
1½ cups (350ml) milk
6 oz (175g) skinless cod
   or haddock fillet

What you do

1 **Peel** the onion and **slice** it finely.

2 Peel the garlic clove and **chop** it finely.

3 **Melt** the butter in a large saucepan. **Fry** the onion and garlic over low heat until the onion is soft, but not brown. This will take about 5 minutes.

4 Add the oregano, cumin, salt, pepper, rice, frozen vegetables, and stock. Bring to a **boil**. Reduce the heat and **simmer** gently for about 30 minutes.

5 In a small bowl, blend the cornstarch with 4 tbsp of milk. Once blended, add the remaining milk.

6 Cut the cod or haddock fillet into chunks and add them to the saucepan. Cook for about 4 minutes.

7 Stir the cornstarch mixture to make sure that it is smooth, then add it to the saucepan, stirring all the time. Continue stirring and cook for about 3 minutes, until the mixture thickens.

8 Ladle the soup into bowls and serve immediately.

ADDED EXTRAS

In Ecuador, the soup is served with chopped hard-boiled eggs, **grated** cheese, chopped peanuts, and chopped parsley on top.

19

Jolloff Rice (Sierra Leone)

This popular party dish is cooked throughout West Africa. It is often served at the meal following a wedding, or on other important family occasions such as birthday parties. People adapt the recipe according to the number of guests they are entertaining. You can add more rice to make the food feed more people.

What you need

1 large onion
1 red chili pepper
½ cup (100ml) peanut oil
1 lb (500g) chicken pieces, stewing beef, or lamb
2 tbsp tomato **purée**
1½ tsp fresh thyme or a large pinch of dried thyme
Salt and pepper
½ cup (100g) long grain rice
½ cup (200ml) plus ¼ cup (100 ml) water

What you do

1 **Peel** and **slice** the onion finely.

(!) 2 Cut the chili pepper in half lengthwise, remove the seeds, and then **chop** it. Always wash your hands with soap after you have handled chili peppers.

(!) 3 Heat the oil in a saucepan. Add a little of the meat and **fry** it for a few minutes, until brown on all sides.

4 Take the meat out of the pan, put it into a warm dish, and fry the rest of the meat, in batches, until it is all browned. It does not have to be cooked all the way through. Set aside and keep warm.

(!) 5 Put the onion and pepper into the pan that you used for the meat. Fry over low heat for about 10 minutes.

(!) 6 Add tomato purée, thyme, salt, pepper, and ¼ cup (100ml) of water. Allow the mixture to **boil**.

7 Return the meat to the pan and **simmer** for about 20 minutes, or until the meat is **tender**. You may need to add a bit more water if the mixture looks dry.

8 Add the rice and ½ cup (200ml) of water to the stew. Let it simmer for about 15 minutes, stirring often. Add a little more water if it seems to be drying out. Once the rice is tender, the dish is ready to serve.

Makaronada (Greece)

This is a Greek version of macaroni and cheese. Like Roman Catholics, members of the Greek Orthodox Church often do not eat meat during Lent, the time when Christians remember the story of how Jesus spent 40 days fasting in the wilderness.

What you need

1¼ cups (300ml) milk
4 tbsp (50g) butter
1 cup (100g) flour
3 eggs
½ cup (125g) macaroni
Salt and pepper
½ cup (125g) cheddar cheese

What you do

(!) 1 Warm the milk, but do not let it **boil**.

(!) 2 **Melt** the butter in another saucepan.

3 Add the flour to the melted butter a little at a time, stirring all the time. Keep the heat under the saucepan low.

4 Add the milk to the flour and butter mixture, a little at a time. Keep stirring so that there are no lumps. When the sauce is thick and creamy, let it cool.

5 Break two of the eggs into a bowl. Using a spoon, lift out the yolks. Mix them into the sauce, along with the other, whole egg. You do not need the spare egg whites in this recipe.

6 **Preheat** the oven to 425°F (220°C).

(!) 7 Bring a large pan of water to a boil, add the macaroni, and cook it until it is soft. This will take about 10 minutes.

8 Carefully **drain** the macaroni and add it to the sauce. **Season** with salt and pepper.

9 Put half the macaroni and sauce in an **ovenproof** dish of about 6- x 9-in. (16- x 23-cm).

10 **Grate** the cheese. Spread half of the grated cheese over the macaroni. Layer the rest of the macaroni and sauce over this and **sprinkle** the top with the remaining cheese.

11 **Bake** for about 20 minutes, until the surface of the makaronada is golden.

WHITE SAUCE

The flour-and-milk sauce is usually known by its French name, which is *béchamel* sauce. If lumps form, push the sauce through a **sieve**, mix it in a blender, or **whisk** it with an electric whisk. Do this before adding the eggs. If the sauce is too thick, just add more milk.

P anut Sauc for Chick n (Uganda)

This sauce is eaten with roasted chicken on special occasions, such as birthday parties, wedding receptions, or other family celebrations. The recipe makes enough sauce for a 3 lb (1.5kg) chicken. In Africa it is often made with freshly roasted peanuts.

What you need

1 large onion
2 tbsp vegetable oil
8 oz (227g) can chopped tomatoes (with their juice)
4 tbsp crunchy peanut butter
1 cup (240ml) milk
Salt and pepper
3 lb (1.5kg) roasted chicken, sliced

What you do

(!) **1** **Peel** and **chop** the onion finely.

(!) **2** Heat the oil in a large saucepan and **fry** the onion until it is golden.

3 Add the tomatoes, peanut butter, milk, and a pinch of salt and pepper. Stir everything together.

4 Cover with a lid and **simmer** for about 20 minutes.

5 Check the sauce regularly and stir it to make sure that it does not burn. Add a little water if the sauce seems to be getting too dry.

6 Serve the warm sauce with **slices** of roasted chicken.

Mancha Manteles (Mexico)

Mancha manteles is a Mexican dish. Its name means "tablecloth stainer," and you will see why when you serve it! It is usually made in midsummer, when Christians celebrate the Festival of Corpus Christi.

What you need

14 oz (400g) lean pork
   tenderloin
2 tbsp vegetable oil
14 oz (400g) chicken pieces
4 mild chili peppers
1/2 of a red pepper
2 tbsp (30g) flaked almonds
1 tbsp sesame seeds
1 tbsp white wine vinegar
7 oz (200g) canned
   tomatoes
1 cinnamon stick
2 apples
1 unripe banana
140g canned, unsweetened
   pineapple, **drained**
¾ cup (200 ml) water

What you do

1 Cut the pork into four pieces.

(!) 2 Heat ¾ cup (200ml) water in a pan. Add pork and let it cook slowly.

(!) 3 Meanwhile, heat the oil in a frying pan and **fry** the chicken until it is brown on all sides, but not cooked through.

4 Add the chicken to the saucepan with the pork. Keep the oil in the frying pan to use again later.

(!) 5 Cut the chili peppers in half lengthwise, remove the seeds, and then **chop** them finely. Always wash your hands after you have handled chili peppers.

6 Remove the seeds from the red pepper and chop it into small pieces.

7 Put the almonds, sesame seeds, chili peppers, and red pepper in the frying pan and fry them, stirring all the time, until the almonds start turning brown.

8 Add the vinegar and tomatoes to the frying pan. Cook for another 3 minutes before putting the red pepper mixture into the saucepan with the chicken and pork.

9 Add the cinnamon stick and enough water to almost cover the mixture.

10 **Peel** and chop the apples and banana. Remove the apple core. Fry the fruit in the leftover oil for a few minutes until lightly browned. Add the pineapple.

11 Put the cooked fruit in the pan with the chicken and pork. Cover with a lid and **simmer** for 30 minutes. Remove the cinnamon stick before serving.

Pumpkin Pie (United States)

Americans make this sweet, spiced pie to celebrate Thanksgiving. This festival dates back to 1621, when the early settlers in New England brought in the first harvest in their new country.

What you need

1 tbsp flour
9-in. (300g) ready-made pie crust dough
2 lb (1kg) fresh pumpkin
¾ cup (80ml) milk
3 eggs
½ cup (125g) sugar
½ tsp ground nutmeg
½ tsp ground ginger
½ tsp ground cinnamon

What you do

1 **Preheat** the oven to 375°F (190°C).

2 **Sprinkle** flour over a clean work surface. Roll out the **dough** until you have a circle about 12 in. (30 cm) wide.

3 Use the pastry to line a 9-in. (20-cm), round pie pan. Prick the base of the dough with a fork.

4 Put a 12-in. (30-cm) piece of **baking parchment** into the pie dough. Fill it with any large, dried beans. This stops the pastry from puffing up in the oven.

(!) 5 Put the pan in the oven and **bake** the pastry for about 15 minutes. Then remove the beans and paper.

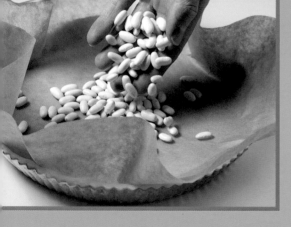

6 Cut the pumpkin into segments, remove the **peel** and seeds, **chop**, and **rinse** 1 lb (500g) of the flesh.

(!) 7 Place the prepared pumpkin in a covered **colander** over a pan of **boiling** water and **steam** it for about 20 minutes, until it is very soft.

8 Put the pumpkin in a bowl with the milk and mash it. Let it cool.

9 **Whisk** the eggs, sugar, nutmeg, ginger, and cinnamon together and mix them into the pumpkin mixture.

(!) 10 Spread the pumpkin mixture into the pie pan. Bake it for about 40 minutes, or until filling has set. Serve hot or cold with whipped cream or vanilla ice cream.

CANNED PUMPKIN

You can use a 1 lb (500g) can of pumpkin instead of fresh pumpkin in this recipe. If you do use canned pumpkin, you can skip steps 6–8 in the recipe.

Tamil Rice Harvest Pudding (Sri Lanka)

This dish is made by the Tamil people of Sri Lanka to celebrate the rice harvest. Traditionally, it is made only from the purest white rice and freshest milk, as the pudding is an offering to the gods. It is cooked in a special pot, early in the morning, so that the first rays of the sun will strike the milk as it begins to **boil**.

What you need

2½ cups (600ml) whole milk

½ cup (125g) long grain rice

1 short stick of cinnamon

A pinch of crushed cardamom seeds

1 ripe banana

A handful of raisins, dates, or golden raisins

½ cup (60g) soft brown sugar

What you do

1 Put the milk in a nonstick saucepan.

(!) **2** Add the rice, cinnamon, and cardamom and place it over low heat. Bring it to a boil.

3 Let the rice **simmer** for an hour. Stir occasionally so that no rice grains stick to the bottom of the pan and burn.

4 When the rice has **absorbed** all the milk, test 1 or 2 grains to see if they are soft all the way through. If the rice is not ready, add a little more milk and simmer a little longer.

5 **Peel** and **slice** the banana. Add it to the rice. Add the dried fruit and sugar and stir well.

6 Remove the pudding from the heat and let sit for about 20 minutes, stirring occasionally to prevent a skin from forming on top. This pudding can be eaten hot or cold.

Crêpes (France)

The Christian fast of Lent starts on a Wednesday. The day before is called Shrove Tuesday. Traditionally, people used up all the rich foods they had on Shrove Tuesday before the Lenten fast began. This is why Shrove Tuesday is sometimes called *Mardi Gras* (or Fat Tuesday). Pancakes, or *crêpes*, were an easy way to use up eggs and milk or cream.

What you need

2 cups (250g) flour
A pinch of salt
2 eggs
¼ cup (60g) butter
2¼ cups (500ml) milk

What you do

1 In a mixing bowl, mix the flour and salt together.

2 Break the eggs into another bowl and **beat** them well.

(!) 3 **Melt** the butter in a frying pan.

4 Make a **well** in the flour and pour the beaten eggs into it.

5 Add the milk and about two-thirds of the melted butter. Leave the rest of the butter in the pan for frying the crêpes.

6 Beat the mixture together to make the **batter** smooth. Let this stand for about an hour.

7 Add a little of the remaining melted butter to the base of a nonstick omelette pan. Place the pan over low heat.

(!) **8** When the butter starts to smoke, add a spoonful of crêpe mixture to the pan. Tip the pan from side to side so that as much of the base as possible is covered by the mixture. Cook for about a minute, until the crêpe bubbles, and then use a nonstick **spatula** to flip the crêpe over and cook the other side.

9 Slide the crêpe on to a warm plate and cover it with wax paper while you make the rest of the crêpes, one at a time.

TASTY FILLINGS

For a savory meal, make a filling for your crêpe using mushrooms, cheese, or ham. For sweet pancakes, try fresh lemon juice and sugar, or jam and cream cheese.

Santa Lucia Cakes (Sweden)

Swedish people serve these special cakes on Santa Lucia's Day, December 13. Saint Lucia was an early Christian. Many of her fellow Christians went into hiding because the Romans wanted to punish them for their faith. Saint Lucia bravely took food to them.

What you need

5 tbsp (75g) butter
2 pinches of saffron
1¼ cups (300ml) plus 3 tbsp milk
7 cups (700g) bread flour
1 packet yeast
½ cup (115g) sugar
A pinch of salt
2 beaten eggs
A handful of raisins

What you do

1 **Melt** the butter slowly in a small pan.

2 In another pan, put the saffron in 1¼ cups (300ml) of milk. Warm until **tepid**.

3 Mix the flour, **yeast**, sugar, and salt in a warm bowl, and make a **well** in the center.

4 Pour in the warm milk and saffron, the melted butter, and one **beaten** egg into the well. Stir to form **dough**.

5 **Knead** the dough on a floured board for about 10 minutes. Add more flour to the mixture if the dough becomes too sticky.

6 Put the dough in a warm place and cover it with plastic wrap. Leave for about 90 minutes to rise.

7 Add the raisins and knead the dough again. Divide into 24 evenly-sized pieces. Roll each into a sausage shape.

8 Cover a baking tray with **baking parchment**. Curl the dough pieces to make *S* or *C* shapes. Place them on a tray. Leave them to rise for another 30 minutes.

9 **Preheat** the oven to 425°F (220°C). Make a **glaze** by mixing 3 tbsp of milk with the other beaten egg. Let it stand for 5 minutes, then brush it over the buns.

(!) 10 **Bake** the buns for around 10 minutes, until they are golden brown. Cool them on a cooling rack.

Parkin (England)

This ginger cake is eaten in England at Bonfire Night parties on November 5. The celebration reminds people about Guy Fawkes, a man who took part in a plot to kill King James I and blow up the Houses of Parliament on November 5, 1605. Fawkes was caught, and people have always remembered the story by building bonfires and setting off fireworks on this day.

What you need

4 tbsp (50g) butter
¾ cup (150g) golden syrup
½ cup (100g) molasses
2 cups (200g) flour
1 cup (250g) old-fashioned oatmeal
¼ cup (50g) sugar
3 tsp ground ginger
1 egg, **beaten**
1½ tsp baking soda
2 tbsp milk

What you do

1 Preheat the oven to 325°F (170°C).

2 Grease a nonstick, square 8- x 8-in. (20- x 20-cm) cake pan with some butter.

(!) 3 Melt the butter, golden syrup, and molasses together in a large saucepan until they are runny. Allow the mixture to cool a little.

4 Stir in the flour, oatmeal, sugar, ginger, and egg.

5 In a separate bowl, mix the baking soda and milk. Add them to the mixture.

(!) 6 Pour the mixture into the cake pan and **bake** it for about 50 minutes.

7 Turn the oven off, keep the door closed, and leave the cake in the oven for another 35 minutes. The parkin will sink a little in the middle of the pan.

8 Cut the parkin into equal squares as soon as it is cool enough to eat.

Cape Malay Milk Tart (South Africa)

This recipe originally comes from Malaysia, and it is made by Malay families who live in the southeast Asian country of South Africa. It is a traditional wedding dish. The tart can be eaten warm or cold.

What you need

1 tbsp plus ½ cup flour
9-in. (300g) ready-made pie pastry
2¼ cups (500ml) milk
1½ tsp vanilla extract
2 eggs
¼ cup (60g) sugar
A pinch of ground cinnamon (optional)

What you do

1 **Preheat** the oven to 325°F (170°C).

2 **Sprinkle** 1 tbsp flour on a work surface and roll out the pastry to make a circle about 14 in. (35 cm) across.

3 Use the pastry to line a nonstick 8-in. (20-cm) pie pan. Trim off the extra pastry and prick the base of the pastry with a fork.

4 Put a 12-in. (30-cm) piece of **baking parchment** into the pastry case. Fill it with large, dried beans. This will stop the pastry from puffing up in the oven.

5 Put the pan in the oven and **bake** the pastry for about 15 minutes. Remove the beans and paper.

6 Warm the milk in a nonstick pan and add the vanilla **extract**.

7 In another nonstick pan, mix the flour with a little of the milk and vanilla mixture, stirring all the time, until you have a smooth **paste**.

! **8** Slowly heat the paste, adding the warm milk a little at a time, stirring so that no lumps form. When all the milk has been added, add the cinnamon if you are using it.

9 Let the sauce **simmer**, stirring until it thickens. This should take about 5 minutes. Let it cool.

10 **Beat** the eggs with the sugar and gradually add them to the milk sauce mixture, stirring all the time.

11 Pour the milk sauce mixture into the pie crust and bake for about 25 minutes.

Honey Cake (Israel)

This honey cake is made for *Rosh Hashanah*, a festival that is celebrated in the fall and marks the beginning of the Jewish New Year. It is supposed to symbolize a sweet start to the New Year.

What you need

2 cups (200g) flour
A pinch of salt
3 tsp baking powder
1½ tsp apple pie spice
¼ cup (50g) sugar
4 eggs
1¼ cups (250ml) honey
5 tbsp (75ml) vegetable oil
1½ tsp instant coffee
   dissolved in ½ cup (100ml)
   hot water
½ cup (80g) walnuts or
   almonds

What you do

1 **Preheat** the oven to 325°F (170°C).

2 Mix flour, salt, baking powder, and apple pie spice in a large bowl.

3 **Whisk** the sugar and eggs together until they are thick and light-colored.

4 Whisk in the honey, vegetable oil, and coffee.

5 Add this mixture and the nuts to the flour mixture.

6 **Grease** an 8-in. (20-cm) round cake pan with a little butter, then pour the mixture into it. **Bake** for about 1 hour. Toward the end of that time, check that the cake is not getting too brown around the edges. If it is, turn the oven down and cover the cake with aluminum foil until it is cooked through.

7 You can check if the cake is cooked by pushing a toothpick into its center. If the toothpick comes out with crumbs on it, the cake is not quite done. If it is clean, the cake is ready to come out of the oven.

8 Let the cake cool in its pan for about 15 minutes. Turn it out onto a cooling rack to cool completely.

Burfi (India)

Divali is the Hindu festival of light and takes place in the fall. People decorate their homes and the streets with lights, have fireworks displays, and share a family celebration. Indian-style sweets, called *burfi*, are a favorite at Hindu festivals.

What you need

1 cup (200g) creamed coconut
¼ cup (40g) butter
1½ tsp cardamom powder
A few strands of saffron (optional)
1½ cups (150g) sugar
2 tbsp flaked almonds

What you do

1 Put the creamed coconut in a bowl over a pan of water.

2 Add 2 tbsp butter, the cardamom, the saffron, and the sugar.

3 Place the pan over very low heat and allow the creamed coconut and butter to **melt**.

4 Keep this mixture over the heat for 10 minutes, stirring it all the time.

5 Melt the remaining butter in a small pan. **Grease** a shallow dish, such as an 8-in. (20-cm) square cake pan, with a little of the butter.

6 Pour the mixture into the greased cake pan and **sprinkle** almonds over it.

7 Allow the *burfi* to cool, and then cut into small pieces.

Further Information

Here are some more books that will tell you about festival foods around the world.

Books

Cook, Deanna. *The Kids' Multicultural Cookbook*. Charlotte, N.C.: Williamson Publishing, 2003.

Jones, Lynda. *Kids Around the World Celebrate!* Chichester, U.K.: John Wiley and Sons, 1999.

Pandya, Meenal. *Here Comes Diwali*. Wellesley, Mass.: Meera Publications, 2001.

Podwal, Mark. *A Sweet Year: A Taste of the Jewish Holidays*. Toronto, Ontario: Doubleday Books for Young Readers, 2003.

Measurements and Conversions

3 teaspoons=1 tablespoon	1 tablespoon=½ fluid ounce	1 teaspoon=5 milliliters
4 tablespoons=¼ cup	1 cup=8 fluid ounces	1 tablespoon=15 milliliters
5 tablespoons=⅛ cup	1 cup=½ pint	1 cup=240 milliliters
8 tablespoons=½ cup	2 cups=1 pint	1 quart=1 liter
10 tablespoons=⅔ cup	4 cups=1 quart	1 ounce=28 grams
12 tablespoons=¾ cup	2 pints=1 quart	1 pound=454 grams
16 tablespoons=1 cup	4 quarts=1 gallon	

Healthy Eating

This diagram shows you what foods you should eat to stay healthy. Most of your food should come from the bottom of the pyramid. Eat some of the foods from the middle every day. Eat only a little of the foods from the top.

Healthy eating at festival time

Festival foods are made to be eaten on special occasions. Many of the recipes are full of fat and sugar. Enjoy your festival favorites—but remember to leave room for foods that are better for you!

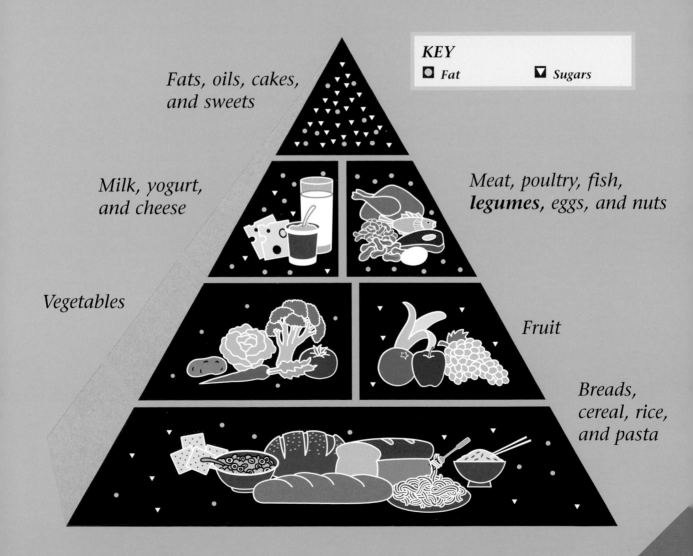

Fats, oils, cakes, and sweets

KEY
◻ *Fat*   ◿ *Sugars*

Milk, yogurt, and cheese

Meat, poultry, fish, legumes, eggs, and nuts

Vegetables

Fruit

Breads, cereal, rice, and pasta

Glossary

absorb soak up

bake cook something in the oven

baking parchment kind of nonstick paper used to line baking trays or cake pans to prevent food from sticking to them

baste moisten with a liquid while baking or roasting

batter mixture of eggs, milk, and flour used for coating fried foods, or making pancakes

beat mix ingredients together, using a fork or whisk

boil cook a liquid on the stove. Boiling liquid bubbles and steams.

chop cut into pieces using a sharp knife

colander bowl-shaped container with holes in it, used for draining vegetables and straining

dough soft mixture of flour and liquid that sticks together and can be shaped or rolled out. It is not too wet to handle, but it is not dry either.

drain allow liquid to run out or away

extract flavoring, such as vanilla or almond extract

fry cook something in oil in a pan

glaze coat food with something to make it look glossy. This can be milk, a mixture of beaten egg and milk, or sugar and water.

grate shred something into small pieces using a grater

grease rub fat over a surface to stop food from sticking

knead press and fold with your hands

legume beans, peas, or seeds from plants that often have pods

melt change from solid to liquid when heated

mince mash and chop something so that it becomes a paste

ovenproof will not crack in the heat of an oven

paste thick mixture

peel remove the skin of a fruit or vegetable; or the skin itself

preheat turn on the oven in advance so that it is hot when you are ready to use it

purée mash, blend, or liquidize food; or the blended food itself

rinse wash under cold running water

season give extra flavor to food by adding salt or pepper

sieve utensil with mesh or holes to separate finer particles from larger ones or solids from liquids

sift shake flour or other powder through a sieve

simmer cook liquid on the stove. Simmering liquid bubbles and steams gently.

slice cut something into thin, flat pieces; or the piece of food itself

slotted spoon large spoon with holes in it that allows you to drain the food as you lift it

soy sauce sauce made from fermented soy beans. Soy sauce is a popular ingredient in Chinese cooking.

spatula flat kitchen utensil used to lift and turn things over

sprig small piece of a plant or herb

sprinkle scatter small pieces or drops onto something

steam cook in steam from boiling water

stigma part of the inside of a flower that picks up pollen. Once pollen is collected on a plant's stigma, the plant can form a seed.

tender soft, but not squashy

tepid only slightly warm, lukewarm

well dip made in the center of flour in a bowl, into which you may pour other ingredients

whisk beat ingredients together to make them light and airy, or the utensil used for doing this

yeast substance used to make bread rise

Index